Mermaids

Coloring Book for Adults & Kids

By

Aada Baldwin

ISBN-13: 978-1523829149

ISBN-10: 1523829141

Introduction

Mermaids were made famous by "Ariel the Mermaid" in Walt Disney's movie, "The Little Mermaid". Mermaids are mythical aquatic creatures with a head and torso of a female human and a tail of a fish.

I hope you enjoy the following 19 hand drawn coloring pages of Mermaids.

Legal Notes

Made in the USA
Columbia, SC
10 September 2018